# PHYSICAL PROCESSES

SERIES EDITOR
**REBECCA HUNTER**

**www.heinemann.co.uk/library**
Visit our website to find out more information about **Heinemann Library** books.

To order:
☎ Phone 44 (0) 1865 888066
🖹 Send a fax to 44 (0) 1865 314091
🖥 Visit the Heinemann Bookshop at www.heinemann.co.uk/library to browse our catalogue and order online.

First published in Great Britain by Heinemann Library, Halley Court, Jordan Hill, Oxford OX2 8EJ, part of Harcourt Education. Heinemann is a registered trademark of Harcourt Education Ltd.

Produced for Heinemann Library by Discovery Books Ltd
Editorial: Nick Hunter and Jennifer Tubbs
Design: Ian Winton
Production: Viv Hichens
Picture research: Maria Joannou

Originated by Ambassador Litho Ltd
Printed in Hong Kong, China by Wing King Tong

ISBN 0 431 17442 3 (hardback)
06 05 04 03 02
10 9 8 7 6 5 4 3 2 1

ISBN 0 431 17446 6 (paperback)
07 06 05 04 03
10 9 8 7 6 5 4 3 2 1

**British Library Cataloguing in Publication Data**
Hunter, Rebecca
    Physical processes. - (Explore Science)
    530
A full catalogue record for this book is available from the British Library.

**Acknowledgements**
The publishers would like to thank the following for permission to reproduce photographs: Ambassador: page **41**; Bruce Coleman: page **33**; Corbis: pages **14**, **26**, **27**;  NASA: pages **40**; Oxford Scientific Films: page **29**; Photodisc: pages **4**, **15**, **18**, **22**, **31**, **36**, **37**, **44**; Rupert Horrox: page **6**; Science Photo Library: pages **9**, **12**, **13**, **16**, **20**, **21**, **23**, **25**, **30**, **32**, **34**, **38**, **39**, **42**, **43**; Trevor Clifford: pages **7**, **8**, **10**, **11**, **17**, **19**, **24**, **28**.

Cover photograph of an astronaut reproduced with permission of Science Photo Library.

The publishers would like to thank Angela Royston for her contributions to the text of this book.

Every effort has been made to contact copyright holders of any material reproduced in this book. Any omissions will be rectified in subsequent printings if notice is given to the publishers.

Any words appearing in the text in **bold**, like this, are explained in the glossary.

# Contents

# Physical processes

Our world is surrounded by **forces**. The force of **gravity** keeps our planet Earth in **orbit** around the Sun. It also holds all of us on the surface of the planet. Earth acts as a giant **magnet** and **electricity** lights our homes and powers our televisions and computers. We experience the world around us through sound and light. We call these things physical processes and the study of them is called physics. But where do all these forces come from and how do they work? To find the answers we have to look at the physical properties of **matter** and **energy**.

### What is electricity?

Electricity is one kind of energy. To understand electricity, first you have to know what **atoms** are. All matter is made up of atoms. Atoms are incredibly tiny. Something as small as a grain of sand contains millions of atoms. **Electrons** are even smaller! An electron is a tiny particle in an atom. We get electricity when electrons leave their atoms and flow from one place to another. We call this flow of electrons an electric **current** and the type of electricity produced, current electricity.

Electricity is very useful, but can also be dangerous. **Mains electricity** is very powerful. If it flows through your body it will give you an electric shock that could kill you. Never touch anything that might carry an electric current such as bare electrical wires.

These bright colourful signs are lit by electricity. Most of the machines we rely on use electrical energy to make them work.

## Electricity

We use electricity for light, heat and to make things work. Televisions, videos, dishwashers, washing-machines, kettles and cookers are machines in your home that use electricity to work. In the street, traffic lights and street lights use electricity. Telephones, computers and faxes all use electricity to send messages.

## Electricity in the home

Current electricity for the home is made in power stations. Power stations turn huge engines called turbines to make electricity. It is then sent along wires to buildings in towns and cities. The wires run inside the walls, under the floors and in the ceilings. One set of wires carries electricity for the lights. A **switch** on the wall lets you turn each light off and on. Another set of wires goes to sockets in the wall. When you push the plug of a machine into the socket, electricity flows through the plug and along the cable to the machine.

## Batteries

A **battery** has chemicals inside it. They make a small amount of electricity. A battery stores this electricity. Mobile phones, toys and torches, use batteries for the electricity they need to work. These batteries are called dry batteries or dry cells.

Many devices use batteries to give them the electricity they need to work. Batteries are useful because they are safe and they are easy to carry around.

## Exploring further – Biographies

The Heinemann CD-ROM can tell you more about batteries and the man who invented them. Follow this path: Contents > Biographies > Alessandro Volta

# Electric circuits

**Electricity** needs to flow around in a circle. This is called an electrical **circuit**. It is made up of different bits, called **components**. Each component is joined to the next one with wire. The electricity flows through the wire and the components. For electricity to flow through the circuit there must be no gaps or breaks in it.

## Components in a circuit

Simple circuits usually have four components:

- a **battery**

  Every circuit must get electricity from somewhere. A simple circuit gets it from a battery. A circuit only needs one battery to work. But you can join two or more batteries together to get more power.

- connectors

  Connectors are usually metal wires. Wires connect all the components in a circuit. They let electricity flow from one component to the next.

- a **switch**

  A switch is a device that can join up or break the circuit. When the switch is on, the circuit is complete and electricity flows. When the switch is off, the circuit is broken so no electricity flows.

- and something that uses electricity, such as a light bulb.

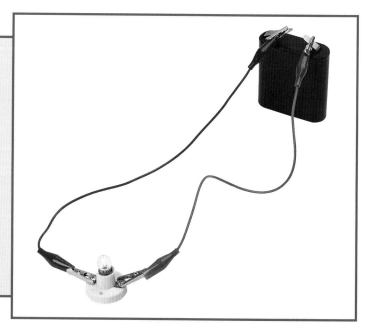

This is one of the simplest circuits. One **terminal** of the battery is connected by a wire to one terminal of the bulb. A second wire is then connected to the battery and joined to the other terminal of the bulb. Electricity flows through the circuit and the bulb lights up.

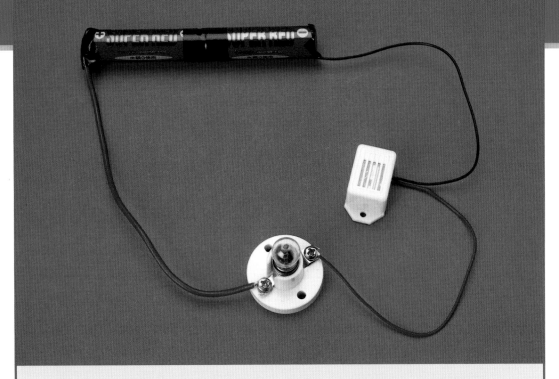

This circuit has two batteries. They provide twice as much electricity as one battery. The circuit also has two components that use electricity – a buzzer and a bulb.

## Other components

Every circuit needs something that uses up electricity to make it work. In a simple circuit, this can be a bulb that uses electricity to make light, or a buzzer that uses electricity to make sound, or a motor that uses electricity to move it. The bulb, the buzzer and the motor are components.

## Voltage

We measure electric **current** in **volts**. The 'volt' is named after Alessandro Volta, who invented batteries. The voltage drives the electric current; the higher the **voltage**, the stronger the electric current. A torch battery has a voltage of 1.5 volts whereas a car battery has 12 volts. Some animals can produce electricity to stun their prey. The electric eel produces a voltage of up to 600 volts! The voltage of **mains electricity** is 240 volts.

## Exploring further – Circuit symbols

A **circuit diagram** is a drawing of a circuit. Find out how to draw a circuit diagram and learn the symbols used all over the world. Follow this path on the CD-ROM: Exploring > Electricity > Circuit Diagrams

# Conductors and insulators

**Conductors** are things that let **electricity** flow through them easily.
**Insulators** are things that block the flow. Most electrical wires are made of copper inside a plastic cover. Copper is a metal that conducts electricity well. Plastic does not conduct electricity at all; it is an insulator. The plastic cover means you can touch the electric wire without getting a shock.

This plastic toothbrush is being used to test whether plastic conducts electricity. If it does, the bulb will light up. If the bulb does not light up then plastic stops the electricity flowing and so is a good insulator.

## Good conductors

All metals conduct electricity, but some metals are better than others. Copper, aluminium, gold and silver are very good conductors. Silver conducts electricity better than copper does, but silver is too expensive to use for electrical wiring.

**Thomas Edison**

Thomas Edison was an American inventor. He made more than 1,000 inventions. One of them was the electric light bulb. Until then people had used candles or oil or gas lamps to give them light. Edison worked hard to find a material that would resist the flow of electricity but not block it completely. He finally used a cotton thread. He also invented a way of supplying electricity to people's homes, and light **switches** so that they could use the new light bulbs.

## Good insulators

Plastic, rubber, wood and glass are all good insulators. Electrical wires are covered in plastic and plugs and sockets are made of plastic for the same reason. The plastic insulates your fingers from the electricity flowing through the inside of the plug.

## Resistors

Some things let electricity flow, but only just! We call them resistors because they resist the flow of electricity. When electricity flows through a resistor, some of the electrical **energy** is changed to heat energy. So the resistor becomes hot.

**How does a light bulb work?**

A light bulb is a kind of resistor. The electricity has to pass through a very thin wire in the middle of the bulb. We call it a **filament**. The filament resists the flow of electricity. It becomes so hot it glows and gives out light.

Look inside a clear light bulb. The fine wire in the centre is the filament. Each end of the filament joins to one **terminal** on the bottom of the bulb.

## Exploring further – Generators

A machine called a generator turns movement into electricity. To learn more about this, follow this path on the CD-ROM: Digging Deeper > Electricity and magnetism > Generators

# Changing circuits

The simplest **circuit** we can make has a **battery**, something that uses **electricity** and wires to connect them. A **switch** can be added to turn the electricity on or off. Other **components** can also be added or taken away, and they will affect the circuit in different ways.

### Adding another component

If you add another bulb, or a buzzer or motor to a simple circuit you add another component that uses electricity. So each component gets less electrical **energy**. If you add another bulb, each bulb will be dimmer than one bulb on its own. The more bulbs you add, the dimmer they all become. Adding a buzzer or a motor makes the bulb dimmer too.

### Adding another battery

If you add another battery to the circuit, you increase the amount of electrical energy flowing through it. Two batteries and one bulb will make the bulb shine brighter than one battery did. Two batteries and two bulbs will make each bulb shine just like one bulb did with one battery. But do not add too many batteries to a circuit! If you do, the bulb or other component will get too much electrical energy and will burn out or 'blow'.

These circuits are the same, except that one circuit has one bulb and the other has two bulbs. The bulb on its own is brighter than each of the two bulbs in the other circuit.

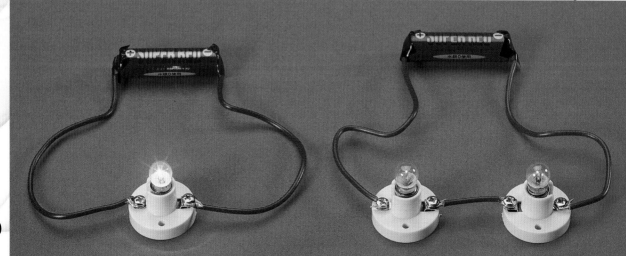

These circuits are the same, except that one circuit has one battery and the other has two batteries. The bulbs in the circuit with one battery are dimmer than the bulbs which are powered by two batteries.

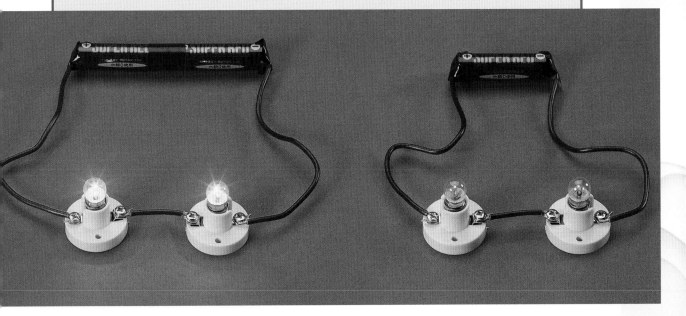

## Changing the wires

Changing the length or thickness of a wire makes a difference to your circuit. You can experiment by using the same battery and bulb and changing only the wires. The longer the wire, the dimmer the light will be.

## Fuses

A **fuse** protects a machine from being burnt out. Electric plugs have a fuse inside them. If the **current** passing through the plug is stronger than the fuse, the fuse burns out. It melts and breaks the circuit. The fuse burns out instead of the machine burning out.

### Exploring further – Fuses

Look at the table of fuses in the Key Ideas bank on the CD-ROM. This shows the fuses that should be used with different machines and electrical appliances. Follow this path: Contents > Key Ideas > Electricity

# Static electricity

There is another type of **electricity** that does not flow along as a **current**. This is **static electricity**. This was the very first form of electricity to be discovered.

We have seen how the flow of **electrons** in **atoms** cause an electric current to flow. Electrons have a negative **electrical charge**. Atoms also contain **protons** which have a positive electrical charge. In an atom the positive and negative charges cancel each other out so the whole atom is neutral – it has no charge at all.

## Static charges

Sometimes electrons are attracted from the atoms in one material to those in another. Have you ever noticed that sometimes when you comb your hair it sticks out from your head? Electrons move from your hair to the comb. The comb, which now has more electrons than before, has a negative electric charge. Your hair, which has lost electrons, has a positive electric charge. Opposite charges are attracted to each other making your hair stick up towards the comb. The build-up of electric charges as they move from one place to another is what causes static electricity.

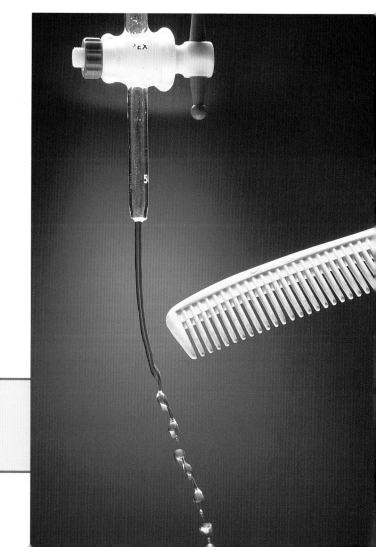

The water is being attracted to the electrically charged comb.

Electricity lights up the sky in a flash of lightning! At any one time, around 100 lightning flashes a second are being produced from about 2000 thunderstorms world-wide.

## Lightning

Lightning is caused by static electricity being formed in clouds during storms. When ice **particles** are swirled around high inside a cloud, they become charged with static electricity. Air is very resistant to electricity and it takes a lot of energy to send an electric charge through the air. The negative charge that builds up on a cloud during a thunderstorm can reach millions of **volts**. This is enough to strip electrons from the atoms in the air, making a passage along which a lightning bolt can travel, sending an explosion of electrical energy between the cloud and the ground.

 **Exploring further – Biographies**

Find out more about Benjamin Franklin who discovered that lightning was a form of electricity. Follow this path on the CD-ROM: Contents > Biographies > Benjamin Franklin

# Forces and motion

## What is a force?

A **force** is a pull or a push. A force makes something move. If you want to move the mouse for your computer you have to push it or pull it. The mouse moves in the same direction as the force. A force can make something speed up, slow down, change direction or change shape.

## Speeding up and slowing down

If you are pedalling a bicycle and want to go faster, you have to pedal harder. You have to use more force. When you play football you push the ball forward with your foot. The harder you kick the ball, the faster it will move. Which way it goes and how fast it goes depends on the direction and strength of the kick. You can use an arrow to show which way a force is moving and how strong it is.

A force can change the direction of something that is moving. When this tennis player hits the moving ball, he puts a force on it that changes its direction, and sends it back to the other side of the court.

## Changing direction

When you hit a ball, you use force to change which way it is moving. A cricketer or baseball player hits a ball that is moving towards them. The ball then changes direction and moves away from them. A twist is a force that makes something move in a circle. Twisting the lid of a jar or bottle opens the jar. Twisting it the opposite way closes it.

## Forces in balance

Sometimes more than one force acts on an object at the same time. When people push or pull in the same direction, their forces add together to give a much bigger force. But if two forces are acting against each other, the largest force will win. When two teams have a tug of war, each team pulls a rope in the opposite direction. The team which pulls the rope over a line wins. The rope is moved by one force being stronger than the other. Sometimes two forces are equal. When this happens, the two forces balance each other. When two forces are balanced there is no movement in either direction.

This duck is floating because the force of the water pushing it up is equal to the force of **gravity** pulling it down.

## Exploring further – Forces in balance

When architects and engineers design buildings and bridges they have to take account of the forces that will be acting on them. Find out more about this on the CD-ROM by following this path: Digging Deeper > Forces > Forces in balance

# Springs

Most springs are made from coiled metal. The metal is strong but bendy. When the coils of the spring are squashed or stretched by a **force**, the spring pushes back with an equal force. When the force is removed, the spring bounces back to the shape it was before.

When a force pushes against any object, the object always reacts by pushing back with an equal force. But when a force acts on a spring, the spring pushes back *and* changes shape too. The **energy** that makes the spring change shape is stored by the spring. When the force is removed, the spring uses the stored energy to bounce back into shape.

## Useful springs

Springs are used in different ways in furniture, toys, trampolines and in many machines and gadgets, like computers, umbrellas and ball-point pens.

Many things use a spring and a catch. When we open an umbrella, a spring is squashed tight and held by a catch. When we take the catch off, the spring relaxes and the umbrella folds up.

When you pull an **elastic** band, it stretches. When you let it go, it goes back into shape. Things that return to shape after they have been stretched are said to be elastic.

This toy clown jumps out of the box when you open the lid. There is a spring under the clown costume. When you shut the lid, the spring is squashed. When you open the lid, the spring expands again and the clown jumps out.

## Measuring forces

We use an instrument called a forcemeter to measure how strong a force is. A forcemeter has a spring inside it. You can use a forcemeter to measure the pull of **gravity** or some other force on an object. As gravity pulls the object towards the ground, the spring stretches and pulls back with an equal force. A forcemeter measures force in **newtons**. (See page 23.)

Using a forcemeter to drag a book across the desk. The forcemeter will read how much force is needed to move the book.

## Changing shape

Forces can press things together or pull them apart. Squashing and stretching things can make them change shape. If you are making a model from clay, you press and pull the clay to change its shape. Some things squash or stretch more easily than others. It is easy to squash a sponge, because it is filled with air.

### Exploring further – Opposing forces

Several different forces can act on one object at the same time. Find out how on the CD-ROM. Follow this path: Quick Facts > Forces in Action > Opposing Forces

# Friction

Friction is a force that happens when two surfaces rub against each other. The two surfaces stick to each other a little. When car wheels roll along the ground, the surface of the wheels stick to the road. The force of friction acts in the opposite direction to the movement and so slows the car down. When the surfaces that are touching each other are rough, there is more friction. You can see this for yourself when you try to slide along a floor in your socks. The smoother the floor, the faster you can slide. It is hardest to slide on a very rough surface, like a deep carpet.

Skis are smooth and narrow. They are designed to reduce friction and allow skiers to slide easily across the snow.

## Treads

Shoes have treads underneath to help them grip. The treads make the bottom of the shoes rougher. The deeper the treads, the more they 'stick' to the ground. Ballet shoes have no treads, so that dancers can slide their feet as they dance.

Wheels have treads too. Tractor wheels have deep treads so that they can drive through muddy fields. An ordinary car wheel would get stuck in the mud, or spin round without gripping the ground. Tractor wheels are large as well as rough to give them extra grip in the mud.

Bicycle brakes use friction. The rubber pads press against the wheel rims and cause friction that stops the wheels from going round.

## Brakes

Brakes use friction to help a car, bicycle or other vehicle stop. On a bicycle when you pull on a brake, the cable pulls two rubber blocks hard up on the rim of the wheel. Friction between the wheel and the brake blocks slows the bike down.

## Reducing friction

Friction also produces heat **energy**. Sometimes this is a good thing. When your hands are cold, you rub them together. The friction between your hands makes them warm again.

In machinery the friction between moving parts can create too much heat. This causes the parts to wear out quickly and in some cases could start a fire. We can use oil or grease to reduce friction. Oil is put in a car engine to reduce the amount of friction between the moving parts.

### Exploring further – Friction

Find out how different shapes and surfaces can affect the amount of friction. Follow this path on the CD-ROM: Digging Deeper > Forces > Friction

# Resistance and streamlining

It is harder to walk through water than to walk through air. The **particles** of water are pushing back against you. We say they are resisting your movement. Air resists movement too. The faster you move, the greater the resistance. When you ride your bicycle fast, you can feel the air pushing back against your face and body.

## Air resistance

When a leaf falls from a tree, it floats gently down to the ground. **Air resistance** pushes up against the surface of the leaf. The bigger the **surface area**, the greater the resistance. A leaf is so light the pull of **gravity** is not much stronger than the upward force of the air resistance. So the leaf falls slowly.

Parachutists use air resistance to slow down their fall. The open parachute has a very large surface area so it makes a lot of air resistance. This slows the parachute down and the parachutist drops gently to the ground.

A space shuttle uses a parachute to slow it down quickly when it lands. This means that it can land on a shorter runway.

## Streamlining

In order for things to move efficiently though air or water, they need to be **streamlined**. This means they need to have the smallest possible surface area to push against the air or water. Car designers test different shapes in **wind tunnels**. They want to see which shapes cut through the air best. Lorries use spoilers to help the air flow more smoothly over their bulky shapes.

**Water resistance** is stronger than air resistance. Animals that move fast through the water need to be streamlined. Dolphins, sharks and most other kinds of fish are all well streamlined. Their smooth, round heads and long, tapering bodies let the water flow past them more easily. Submarines have the same streamlined shape to help them move faster through the water.

There is no resistance in space because there are no particles of air or water there. So spacecraft flying in space do not need to have streamlined shapes. In fact many **satellites** and spacecraft have aerials, antennae, solar panels and many other bulky things attached to them.

Dolphins can swim quickly through the water. Their streamlined shape means that they can slide through the water without much resistance.

## Exploring further – Streamlining

See how the shape of a car influences how air passes over it. Watch this animation on the CD-ROM. Follow this path: Quick Facts > Resistance and Streamlining > Key Ideas bank

# Gravity

**Gravity** is the **force** that keeps your feet on the ground. Without gravity, you would fly off into space. Gravity is the force that pulls everything towards the centre of the Earth. It works in water, on land and in the air.

## Weight

Your **weight** measures the pull of gravity. A heavy object is being pulled strongly towards the centre of the Earth. A light object is not being pulled so strongly. Things which are the same size do not all weigh the same. A football is lighter than a watermelon of about the same size. A duvet is big, but it does not weigh as much as a computer.

This athlete uses muscle power to push up into the air. Gravity pulls the athlete back down to the ground.

### Sir Isaac Newton (1642–1727)

Sir Isaac Newton was an English philosopher, mathematician and scientist. He made many important discoveries, including the idea of a force called gravity. He realized that the force of gravity, which makes objects fall to the ground, is the same force that keeps the Moon **orbiting** Earth and the planets orbiting the Sun. Many people believe Newton to be the greatest scientist who ever lived. As well as his work on motion and gravity, he investigated light and invented a new system of mathematics, called calculus. The unit of force – the newton – was named after him.

## Newtons

Forces are generally measured in units called **newtons**. Ten newtons are roughly the force needed to move a mass of one kilogram on the Earth. One newton is about the force you would need to lift an apple a metre off the ground. A typical jet engine exerts a force of about 100,000 newtons.

## Escaping gravity

You have to go a long way away from Earth before you escape from the force of gravity. The astronauts who went to the Moon escaped the pull of Earth's gravity. In space they weighed nothing and floated around the spacecraft. But every large object in space has gravity. When the astronauts reached the Moon, they then felt the pull of the Moon's gravity. The largest objects have the strongest pull. The Earth is larger than the Moon and so gravity on Earth is stronger than on the Moon.

Astronauts feel lighter on the Moon than they do on Earth. An astronaut in a space suit who weighs 135 kilograms on Earth, will only weigh 22 kilograms on the Moon.

## Exploring further – Newton's laws

Find out more about Sir Isaac Newton's three laws of motion. Follow this path on the CD-ROM: Digging Deeper > Forces > Newton's laws

# Magnetism

A **magnet attracts** some things but not others. We call this attraction a magnetic force. Things that are attracted to magnets are said to be magnetic. Magnets can attract each other, or push each other away. Some metals are magnetic but some are not. Iron is magnetic and so are things that have iron in them.

## Magnetic poles

A magnet's force is strongest at its ends. The ends are called the poles of the magnet. If you put the poles of two magnets together, they will pull together or push apart. We say they attract each other, or **repel** each other. One end of a magnet is called the north pole and the other end is called the south pole. The north pole of one magnet will be attracted to the south pole of another magnet, but will always repel another north pole.

## Magnetic Earth

Our planet, Earth, is a massive magnet. If you let a magnet swing freely, it will line up so that its south pole is pointing to Earth's magnetic north pole. A **compass** does this. The needle of the compass is a magnet that is free to spin. When you hold the compass steady, the arrow always points north. The end of the arrow is the south pole of the needle.

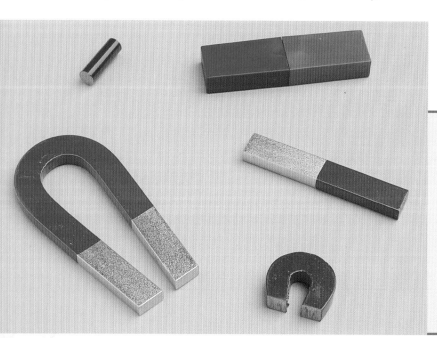

Magnets are made in different shapes, but the most common shapes are a horseshoe or a bar. All magnets attract things made of iron or steel, such as paper clips.

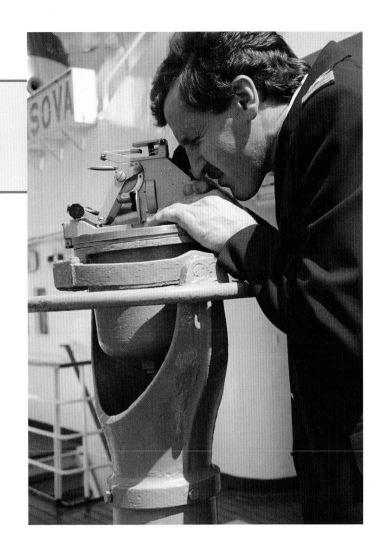

Sailors use a compass to help them find their way across the oceans.

Lodestone, which contains iron, is a naturally magnetic rock. It was used in the first compasses, which may have been in use in China as early as the 5th century BCE. The word **magnetism** comes from Magnesia, a region in Asia Minor where lodestone was found.

## How magnetic force is used

There are many ways in which we use magnetic force. Fridge magnets stick to the fridge because the steel casing of the fridge is magnetic. Magnets are used in the recycling centre to sort out the steel cans from the aluminium ones. Magnets can be used along with other materials. A fridge or freezer needs to be airtight to stay cold. Its door has a rubber strip around the edge which contains tiny magnets. The magnets make the strip cling tightly when the door is shut.

### Exploring further – Electromagnetism

Learn how **electricity** and magnetism are related, and how we use electromagnets, on the CD-ROM. Follow this path: Digging Deeper > Electricity and magnetism > Electromagnets

# Light and sound

## Light from the Sun

The Sun is the natural source of light on Earth. During the day most of our light comes from the Sun. Sunlight is brightest when the Sun is high in the sky and there are no clouds, but the light from the Sun is so strong, it reaches us even when it is cloudy. In the evening, the Sun gets lower and lower in the sky until it drops out of sight. When the Sun has gone, it is dark. Then the only light there is comes from other sources.

The Sun is our main source of light. Even when the Sun is hidden behind a cloud, its light reaches us.

## Other sources of light

At night we use other sources of light, like electric lights, torches, candles and the **stars**. Stars are a natural source of light, but they are so far away that only a tiny bit of light reaches us. The stars are still there in the sky during the day, but the light of the Sun is so bright that we can't see them. The Moon does not create its own light. When it shines at night it is reflecting light from the Sun like a giant mirror.

At night most of our light comes from electric lights. Electric lights are easy and convenient to use.

## Artificial light

Some people burn candles and oil lamps to give them light at night. When anything burns, it gives off light. Fireworks light up the night sky but each one only lasts for a short time. Candles and oil lamps use wicks to stop them burning too fast. The oil or melted wax soaks into the wick and burns bit by bit. In the past, they were often our only way to get light at night.

Electric light is another artificial source of light. An electric light uses **electricity** to heat up a fine wire called a **filament**. The filament is inside a glass bulb. The filament glows brightly for a long time without burning up.

**How fast does light travel?**

Light travels very fast. If you could travel at the speed of light you could travel seven times around the Earth in under a second! The light from the Sun crosses about 150 million kilometres of nearly empty space to reach us in just eight minutes. Light travels through empty space at nearly 300,000 kilometres per second.

## Exploring further – Colour

The white light from the Sun is actually a combination of different colours, called the spectrum. Find out more about the light spectrum on the CD-ROM. Follow this path: Digging Deeper > Sound and light > Colour

# Shadows

Light can pass through some things, but not through others. A material that lets light pass through it is said to be **transparent**. A material which blocks light is **opaque**, creating **shadows**.

## Transparent or opaque?

You can see through a glass window, because light passes straight through the glass. The glass is transparent. Clear plastic and clean water are both transparent.

You cannot see through a brick wall or a wooden door, because light cannot pass through bricks or wood. Many kinds of material, like stone, cardboard and metals, are opaque.

Some materials let some light pass through but you cannot see clearly through them. We call them **translucent**. Tissue paper, coloured and cloudy glass and some kinds of plastic are translucent.

The clear glass vase is transparent. You can clearly see the stalks of the flowers in it. The china vase is opaque. You cannot see the stalks inside it at all. The shadow made by the china vase is much deeper than the shadow of the transparent vase.

## Making shadows

When something blocks the light, it makes a shadow. A shadow is a patch of dimmer light. Opaque objects make the strongest shadows. Translucent objects make weaker shadows. Even a transparent object makes a bit of a shadow, as you can see in the picture above.

## Shape and size of shadows

Light waves always travel along straight paths. You can see straight rays of light when the Sun shines through gaps in broken clouds. A shadow is similar in shape to the object that caused it. The size of the shadow depends on how close the object blocking the light is to the source of the light. When the object is far away from the light source, the shadow is small because little light is blocked out. An object near to the light source will block a lot of light and so make a big shadow.

## Length of shadows

Why are some shadows longer or shorter than others? The length of a shadow changes when the direction of the light changes. If the light is just above and behind the object, the shadow is about the same size as the object. But if the light is overhead, the shadow is shorter. When the light is behind the object, the shadow is longer. You can see this effect outside on a sunny day. In the morning when the Sun is low in the sky, it makes long shadows. As the Sun rises, the shadows get shorter until midday. After midday they slowly become longer until the Sun sets.

 **How does a sundial work?**

In the past, people used sundials to tell the time. A sundial has a pointer that makes a shadow on a dial. The shadow moves around the dial between sunrise and sunset. The shadow tells you what time it is.

 **Exploring further – Shadow portraits**

Have fun making shadow portraits of your family and friends. Find out how on the CD-ROM. Follow this path: Digging Deeper > Sound and light > What is light?

# How we see things

Light hits everything in its path. When it hits something, it bounces off. Wherever you look, light is bouncing off all the things in front of you. Some of the bouncing light reaches your eyes. The eye bends the light so that it forms a picture of the object on the back of your eye. We call this picture an image.

## The human eye

The black circle in the centre of your eye is a hole called the **pupil**. It is covered by the **cornea**. The cornea is **transparent** so light can go straight through it. Light enters your eye through the cornea and the pupil. As it passes through the **lens**, the light bends and makes a clear picture on the back of the eye. The back of the eye is called the **retina**. The retina is covered by nerve endings. They react to light and send the image to your brain. The image on the retina is upside down, but the brain turns it the right way up. The coloured circle around the pupil is called the iris. It is a muscle that can change the size of the pupil. In bright light the iris makes the pupil smaller so that less light enters the eye.

Light enters the eye through the pupil – the black hole in the centre of the eye.

Strong light can damage your eyes. The pupils become smaller in bright light to keep some of the damaging light out. You should shield your eyes from bright light, but in strong sunlight you should wear sunglasses too. You should never look straight at the Sun.

## Binocular vision

Each eye sends a slightly different image to the brain. You can see this for yourself. Close one eye and line up a finger with a distant object. Now, without moving the finger, open the other eye and close the first one. The finger is no longer lined up. This is because each eye sees an object from a slightly different angle and at a slightly different place in its field of vision. The brain forms a three-dimensional image from the two images it receives from the eyes. This is called binocular vision. It allows us to judge how far away an object is.

## Animals' eyes

Each kind of animal has eyes that help it to look for food and watch out for enemies. Many grazing animals, like deer and rabbits, have an eye on each side of their head. They can spot movement in almost every direction. Most birds also have an eye on each side of their head although owls have eyes at the front to help them hunt in the dark.

## Exploring further – Seeing

Our eyes are incredibly clever organs. Find out more about how they work.
Follow this path on the CD-ROM: Quick Facts > How we see things - shadows

# Sound

All sounds are caused by **vibrations**. If you pluck a guitar string the string vibrates. It moves backwards and forwards rapidly and as it does so it bumps into and pushes the air alongside it, sending waves of **energy** through the air.

Sound travels from its source through everything it is in contact with. When something vibrates, the air around it vibrates. Waves of sound move out from the source, like ripples on a pond when a stone is dropped into it. Sound waves can travel through gases, like air; liquids, like water; and many solids, like wooden doors and brick walls.

You can pluck the strings of a guitar to make a range of different notes. When you pluck a string it vibrates. The strings are pulled very tight so that you do not have to use much force to make them vibrate.

## Speed of sound

Sound travels at about 340 metres per second through the air at ground level. This is much slower than light. In fact it is a million times slower! You can see this in action during a thunderstorm. Although the lightning and thunder happen at the same time, you see the lightning several seconds before you hear the thunder.

Sound travels four times as quickly through water as it does through air; it also travels much further. Humpback whales travel long distances from the cold polar seas to warm tropical seas and back. They keep in touch with each other by singing. The song can be heard by other humpback whales hundreds of kilometres away.

Sound travels through most solids. Tiny **particles** in the solid vibrate and pass on the sound. Sound travels through some solids better than through air. It travels through steel fifteen times as fast. When you are waiting for a train, you can often hear the rails vibrating before the noise of the train reaches you through the air. Sound also travels well through the ground. Native Americans used to put their ears to the ground to hear the sound of horses' hooves, before they could hear them in the air.

## Exploring further – Hearing

Find out how we hear sounds using our ears. Follow this path on the CD-ROM:Digging Deeper > Sound and light > How we hear

# Making sounds

Sounds are made in different ways by different things. Engines make a lot of sound when they are working. When a washing-machine is running, you can hear the noise of the motor, the water sloshing backwards and forwards, and the whine of the drum when it spins around fast. The whole machine may shake and rattle as well.

Liquids and gases can **vibrate** too. When you open a bottle of fizzy drink, you can hear the sound of the gas escaping. When something explodes, it makes a loud bang. The air around the explosion vibrates too. Vibrating air carries the sound away from the source for some distance.

A firework display brilliantly combines sound and light in a spectacular way.

## Animal voices

Mammals, frogs and birds make sounds by vibrating vocal cords in their throats, like humans. Birds produce many different notes when they sing. Some can even sing two notes at once and so sing duets all by themselves. Most mammals use sounds to send messages to each other.

Other animals have no voice-box and use other parts of their bodies to make a noise instead. Some fish grind their teeth, while others rub their fins against their bodies. Bees beat their wings very fast to make them hum. Crickets are noisy insects that rub their back legs together to make their own special sound.

## Music

Musical instruments can make many different musical notes in different ways. Stringed instruments, such as violins, cellos, pianos, harps and banjos all use vibrating strings to create musical noises. Drums, cymbals and other percussion instruments are played by tapping or banging a surface. When a drum is tapped with a drum stick, the thin covering on the drum vibrates. Flutes, oboes, trumpets, saxophones and recorders all need air blown into them to make a noise. That's why we call them wind instruments.

## Muffling sound

Some materials absorb the energy of sound and stop the **vibrations** passing through them. Curtains and other fabrics absorb sound. If you put your pillow over your head, you will not hear your alarm clock so well. Recording studios need to stop all sounds from outside the studio coming in. The walls are lined with tiles made of special materials that block even loud noises. We call it sound-proofing.

**Why is there no sound in space?**

Sound waves are carried by **matter**. The matter can be solid, liquid or gas, but something is needed to carry the sound. In space there is no matter, so sound waves cannot move. This means that space is totally silent. The Moon also has no atmosphere there so there is no sound.

## Exploring further – Travelling sound

Learn more about how sound travels through solids, liquids and gases. Follow this path on the CD-ROM: Exploring > Light and sound > How sound travels

# Changing sounds

When you learn to play a musical instrument, such as a recorder, guitar or trumpet, you learn how to make different notes. Some notes are high and others are low. Different instruments produce high and low notes in different ways. An instrument can also be played loudly or softly. Most musical instruments produce separate sounds, called notes. Most sounds are many notes jumbled together. When you press down one key on a piano, you get the pure sound of a single note.

## Low and high sounds

Something that is pulled tight produces a higher sound than something that is loose. When you tune a guitar, you tighten or loosen the strings until you get the right note.

**Pitch** describes how low or high a sound is. The tighter the string, the higher the pitch. A looser string gives a lower note. The top of some drums is a skin stretched over the sides of the drum. When the skin is tightened, the drum makes a higher sound.

You use your fingers to shorten the strings on a guitar. Putting your fingers in particular places will make different notes on each string.

## Loudness

Sound is a kind of **energy**. When you bang a drum, the energy of the blow passes into the drum and makes it **vibrate**. The harder you bang, the more energy you pass on. Loud sounds have got more energy than soft sounds. We measure sounds in **decibels**. A whisper is only about 20 decibels and an alarm clock is about 80 decibels.

## Ear protection

Sounds are louder the closer you are to them. Workers who use loud machines, like road drills and chain-saws, wear earmuffs to protect their ears. The earmuffs absorb most of the sound. When sound reaches 130 decibels, your ears hurt. You feel pain rather than hear sound. This level of sound will immediately damage your ears. Sounds over 165 decibels can kill!

This man has earmuffs to protect his ears from the sound of the saw. Loud sounds contain more energy than soft sounds. Some loud sounds contain so much energy they can damage your ears.

## Acoustics

The study of sound and how it travels is called **acoustics**. Sound waves travel in straight lines from the source of the sound. When they strike objects they may be either reflected or absorbed.

If you stand at a distance from a hard, flat surface, such as the side of a building or a cliff, and shout towards it you will hear the sound of your shout bouncing back to you. This is called an **echo**.

### Exploring further – Pitch

You can find out more about pitch on the CD-ROM. Follow this path: Quick Facts > Changing Sounds - pitch

# Earth and beyond

## Earth in space

For thousands of years people thought that Earth was the centre of the **universe**, and that the Sun, the **stars** and **planets** all moved around it. They were wrong. In the 16th century, Nicolaus Copernicus said that Earth and the other planets circled around the Sun.

### Nicolaus Copernicus (1473–1543)

Nicolaus Copernicus was a Polish **astronomer**. In Copernicus's day, people believed everything else in the sky circled around Earth. This was the view of the Greek astronomer, Ptolemy. For hundreds of years, the church had believed Ptolemy's idea that Earth was at the centre of the Universe. But Copernicus came to believe that Earth spun round on its own axis and, like the other planets, circled around the Sun. He said that Earth was not at the centre of the Universe as people then believed, but that Earth and the other planets moved around the Sun. Fifty years later, Galileo was the first person to use a telescope to study the sky and proved that Copernicus was right.

This is a picture of Galileo Galilei demonstrating his telescope in 1609. He used it to study the movement of the planets. He came to the conclusion that Copernicus was right when he said that Earth was not the centre of the Universe.

## The Solar System

The **Solar System** is all the planets, moons and **asteroids** which **orbit** the Sun. Only the Sun produces light. Everything else in the Solar System reflects light from the Sun. The **gravity** of the Sun is so strong that it keeps Earth, the Moon and everything in the Solar System orbiting around it.

## The planets

Earth is just one of nine planets which move around the Sun. It is the third furthest from the Sun. Earth is unusual among the planets because it is the only one known to support life. Mercury, the smallest planet, is the nearest to the Sun. Next comes Venus, then Earth and then Mars. Beyond Mars are four giant planets: Jupiter, Saturn, Uranus and Neptune. These four planets are mostly made up of gases. Jupiter is the largest. It is more than 1300 times bigger than Earth. The furthest planet from the Sun is Pluto. It is smaller than Earth and, because it is so far from the Sun, much colder.

The planets are very different from each other. The **atmosphere** around each planet is different. And each planet has different length days and years.

*Voyager 1* and *Voyager 2* were both launched by the United States in 1977. These unmanned spacecraft travelled on an epic voyage that took them to the outer planets. They flew past Jupiter in 1979 and Saturn in 1981. It then took a further five years for *Voyager 2* to reach Uranus and another three before it flew past Neptune in 1989. These spacecraft sent back valuable information and photographs.

## Exploring further – Space journey

Take a 'journey' across the Solar System on the CD-ROM. Follow this path:
Digging Deeper > Across the Solar System > Journey map

# The Sun

The Sun is a gigantic ball of hot gas nearly 1.4 million kilometres across. It is so massive that the material in the centre of the Sun has become very compressed. In the centre of the Sun the **atoms** smash into each other with such **force** that they fuse together. Huge amounts of **energy** are given off as this happens. In the Sun this takes the form of heat and light energy. The temperature at the centre of the Sun is incredibly high – about 14,000,000° Celsius.

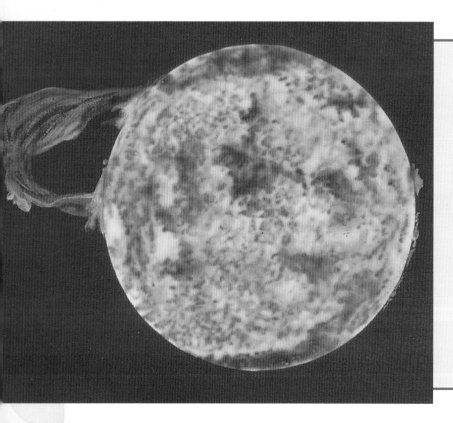

Without the Sun's warmth, there would be no life on Earth. Plants use the Sun's energy to grow. Without plants, animals would have nothing to feed on. Notice the solar flare – an immense jet of flame that sometimes shoots out into space from the Sun.

### ? How big is the Sun?

The Sun is over a million times bigger than Earth. It is so massive, it looks large in the sky even though it is 150,000,000 kilometres away. It takes light, travelling at about 300,000 kilometres per second, just over eight minutes to travel from the Sun to Earth. Earth takes 365 ¼ days to **orbit** the Sun. For three years we have 365 days and ignore the extra ¼ day. But every four years we add an extra day. This is called a leap year.

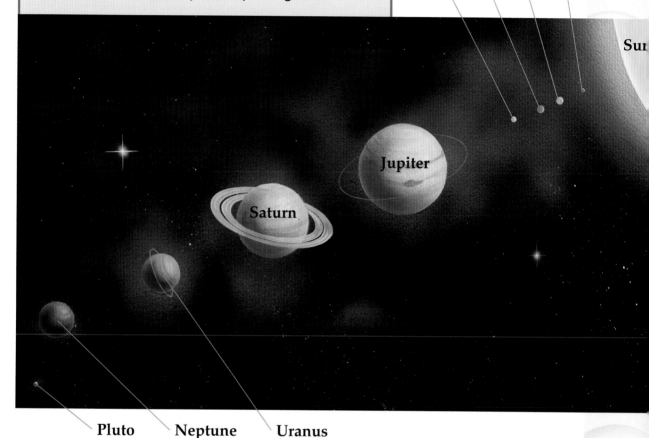

Here you can see the size of planets compared to the Sun. Pluto is the smallest planet. Jupiter is the largest. The Sun is almost 100 times larger than all of the other planets put together.

Mercury

Venus

Earth

Mars

Sun

Jupiter

Saturn

Pluto    Neptune    Uranus

## The death of the Sun

The Sun is like an immense **nuclear** explosion. Its surface is a bubbling, boiling mass of burning gases. It has been burning for five billion years. In about another six billion years it will grow in size to become an even bigger flaming ball, called a red giant. When this happens, the Earth and all the other planets will be burned up and all life destroyed.

## Exploring further – Solar eclipse

During a total eclipse of the Sun, the Sun's light is blocked by the Moon and the Earth loses its source of light. Find out more about what happens during an eclipse. Follow this path on the CD-ROM:
Exploring > The Earth and beyond > The Moon

# The Moon

A moon is a **satellite** that **orbits** a **planet**. Mars has two moons; Earth has one. Jupiter and Saturn have several moons. Our Moon is Earth's nearest neighbour. It is about a quarter the size of Earth, but it looks large in the sky because it is much closer than anything else. In 1969, astronauts travelled the 348,000 kilometres to the Moon and landed on it. It is the only world, other than Earth, that people have visited.

The Moon is made of a rock called basalt. The surface of the Moon is covered with craters and is completely bare. It is covered with fine soil but has no plants and no animals because it has no air and no water. People have to take their own oxygen to breathe and their own food and water. They have to wear space suits to protect them from the rays of the Sun.

On Earth, the **atmosphere** collects some of the heat of the Sun and holds it like a blanket during the night. But the Moon has no gases around it to act like this. During the day, the temperature on the Moon becomes scorching hot, up to 214° Celcius, and at night it drops to a very cold -184° Celcius. But at the Moon's poles, the temperature stays at -96° Celcius during the day and night. Because there is no atmosphere on the Moon, there is no wind and no rain.

The surface of the Moon is scarred by **craters** formed millions of years ago. There is no wind or weather on the Moon and so nothing on the surface changes. Even the footprints left by the first astronauts are still there over 30 years later.

To us on Earth, the Moon appears to change shape because we only see the part of its surface that is lit by the Sun.

The Moon orbits Earth once every 28 days. That is where we get the word 'month' from. It also takes 28 days to spin on its own axis. So the same side of the Moon is always facing Earth. No one knew what the other side of the Moon looked like until a spacecraft flew round it and took photographs.

## Phases of the Moon

The Moon gives off no light of its own. It shines by reflecting the light of the Sun. When the Moon is between Earth and the Sun, the side of the Moon pointing towards us is in **shadow** and we cannot see it from Earth. This is called the New Moon. Just after New Moon, a thin crescent appears on the eastern side of the Moon. Each night the crescent gets a bit bigger. Full Moon is when the whole face of the Moon is lit up by the Sun. After Full Moon the eastern half of the Moon begins to darken. Gradually it becomes a New Moon once more.

### Exploring further – Moving Moon

See what actually happens as the Moon orbits Earth using the animation on the CD-ROM. Follow this path: Contents > Key Ideas > The Earth and beyond

# What do scientists do?

Scientists want to know more about the world and how to look after it. They ask questions about all the things in our world that affect how we live, how comfortable we are and how we keep healthy. For hundreds of years, scientists have studied the plants and animals in the living world and the materials and processes of the physical world, to try and find out why certain things happen.

We all need to understand about science and how a scientist works. To become a good scientist you will need to be curious about the things you use, the things you see and the things that happen around you.

Part of being a scientist is asking questions. Some of these questions can be answered by reading books and using CD-ROMs and the Internet.

Sometimes you will want to find out the answer by doing a scientific investigation. You will need to collect information and use this to try to give an answer to your question. Sometimes our questions are not answered and we need to try again with a different investigation. Once you have collected your information, you need to record it. Then you will need to think about what your results mean and what you can learn from them.

Doing all these things can help you to learn more about the world. When you can understand how important it is to carry out the scientific process correctly, then you will be well on your way to becoming a good scientist.

# Exploring further

Learn more about the amazing physical processes that govern our planet, plus what goes on beyond it in space. The CD-ROM can suggest further areas to explore.

## Weblinks

You can find out more about this area of science by looking at the Weblinks on the CD-ROM. Here is a selection of sites available:

**www.explorescience.com**
An interactive site with plenty of animated activities that teach the young (and not-so-young) about physical processes.

**www.sciencemuseum.org.uk**
The Science Museum in London houses displays on electricity and magnetism. You can visit the museum online at this address.

**spaceplace.jpl.nasa.gov**
The Space Place offers information, games and activities for both children and teachers.

**amazing-space.stsci.edu**
Amazing Space is full of facts and activities based around space. It also includes a gallery with photographs from the Hubble Space Telescope.

**www.4learning.co.uk/weblogic/essentials/science/physical/index.jsp**
Channel 4's 'get physical' area looks at how you can have fun with magnets and springs, find out how gravity works and how movement becomes sound.

**www.opticalres.com/kidoptx.html#LightBasics**
How long does light take to reach us from the Sun? How can we split up white light to make a rainbow effect? The Optics for Kids site reveals the answers!

**www.ncsu.edu/sciencejunction/station/experiments/EGG/egg.html**
A set of three fun home experiments using eggs. What happens to eggs in acid? Can substances pass through the shell? How do forces affect the motion of objects?

## Further reading

*Science of Gravity*, John Stringer, Wayland: 2000
*Electricity and Magnetism*, Chris Oxlade, Heinemann Library, Oxford: 2000
*Sound and Light*, Robert Snedden, Heinemann Library, Oxford: 2000
*Energy, Forces and Motion*, Alistair Smith, Usborne: 2001
*Forces and Motion*, John Graham, Kingfisher: 2001
*Across the Solar System*, Rod Theodorou, Heinemann Library, Oxford: 2000

# Glossary

**acoustics** study of sound and how it travels within a space, such as a room or concert hall

**air resistance** force of the air pushing back against a moving object

**asteroid** large rocks that orbit the Sun in a belt between Mars and Jupiter

**astronomer** person who studies the stars

**atmosphere** layer of gases that surrounds the Earth and some other planets

**atom** one of the tiny particles from which all materials are made

**attract** to pull or cause to move towards

**battery** small, self-contained source of electrical power in a circuit

**BCE** Before Common Era

**circuit** arrangement of conducting wires and components through which electricity flows

**circuit diagram** plan of a circuit which uses symbols to show all the components in a circuit and how they are connected up

**compass** an instrument that shows the direction of magnetic North

**component** a device in a circuit

**conductor** something that allows electricity or heat to flow through it

**cornea** transparent layer covering the eye

**craters** large cavity in the ground or in a planet

**current** the flow of electricity through a circuit; can also refer to the flow of other things, such as water

**decibel** unit used to measure sound

**echo** sound that is reflected from something so you hear it again

**elastic/elasticity** describes something that can return to shape after being stretched or squashed

**electric charge** something that makes some particles exert a force on each other. Charge can be either positive or negative. Opposite charges attract and like charges repel each other.

**electricity** kind of energy used for lighting, heating and making machines work

**electron** negatively charged particle in an atom

**energy** power to provide light or heat or do physical work

**filament** thin wire in a light bulb which glows brightly when electricity passes through it

**force** a push or pull

**friction** rubbing between the surfaces of different objects – it can slow things down or stop them, and create heat

**fuse** strip of metal or thin wire that melts and breaks a circuit when too much current passes through it

**gravity** force of attraction between objects, especially between a very large object such as Earth and other objects near it

**insulator** something that does not allow electricity, or heat, to flow through it

**lens** something that can change the direction of beams of light

**magnet/magnetic** piece of iron that attracts other things that contain iron or steel

**magnetism** force of attraction or repulsion that acts between some materials, such as iron

**mains electricity** electricity that is generated in power stations and supplied to buildings through a nationwide network of wires

**matter** anything that occupies space and has mass

**newton** unit for measuring force

**nuclear** relating to the nucleus of an atom

**opaque** not allowing light to pass through

**orbit/orbiting** path an object follows as it travels around a larger object

**particles** tiny pieces of matter

**pitch** how high or low a sound is

**planet** large object that orbits a star; Earth, for example, is a planet that orbits the Sun

**proton** one of the particles that make up the nucleus of an atom

**pupil** circular opening in the eye through which light enters the eye

**repel** to push away from

**retina** layer inside the eye that contains nerve endings that react to light and send signals to the brain

**satellite** object which moves around a star, planet or moon in an orbit

**shadow** patch of darkness or dim light made when an object blocks light

**Solar System** the Sun together with everything that revolves around it – all the planets, their moons, the asteroids and comets

**star** large, spinning ball of hot, luminous gas in space, like our Sun

**static electricity** electricity which builds up on objects which are rubbed together. For example, your clothes build up static electricity when they rub together.

**streamlined** shape which will move easily through air or water

**surface area** the area of the uppermost layer of something

**switch** device for opening and closing a gap in a circuit, to control whether electricity flows through the circuit

**terminal** place where a wire is connected to a battery or component

**translucent** allowing some light to pass through, but not allowing you to see through clearly

**transparent** allowing light to pass straight through so that you can see through

**universe** space and everything in it

**vibrate/vibrations** very fast but small movements backwards and forwards

**volt/voltage** measure of the force of an electric current; the amount of 'push' given to electrons to make them flow

**water resistance** force of the water pushing back against an object moving through it

**weight** measure of the force of gravity acting on an object

**wind tunnel** apparatus for investigating the flow of air over a vehicle or building

# Index

# Titles in the *Explore Science* series include:

Hardback    0 431 17440 7

Hardback    0 431 17441 5

Hardback    0 431 17442 3

Find out about the other titles in this series on our website www.heinemann.co.uk/library